Debra Kang Dean's *Fugitive Blues* is a collection of brightly colored elegies and odes. Here is the examination of desire and loss, of language and its haunted echoes: "This is / a virtual sound of grief turned / grievance—and that is my grief." Through repetition and syntactic play, Dean produces a rich and sonorous music, as in her meditation on goldfinches: "I was thunked, word-stirred: / *Sunlight, sunlight, bird.*" Dean's vibrant imagery complements her ever shifting landscapes: craters, homesteads, the sky and stars, Japanese Gardens, and beyond. This attention to the art and act of seeing is apparent in her series on symbols: the circle, triangle, and less-than and greater-than signs, which serve as the titles of several poems. Moreover, they provide objects on which Dean fixes her exacting attention. Such experimentally minded gestures juxtapose more lyrical poems of grief, providing a necessary and generous counterbalance. These are smart, elegantly crafted poems that continue to delight and surprise.

—Hadara Bar-Nadav, author of *Lullaby (with Exit Sign)*

Debra Kang Dean's *Fugitive Blues* confronts "this theater under the stars" with evocative poems that combine a microscopic attentiveness to language and to image with a macroscopic sensibility of our cosmic precariousness. Never daunted, Dean trudges through this "ankle-wrenching terrain" where nonetheless we are "word-stirred" by beauty.

—Nathan Hoks, author of *The Narrow Circle*

"Once you know what you're seeing, / the hour of innocence is past," Debra Kang Dean tells us in this remarkable new collection of poems. We see each side of that construction here, the world (and the poet's experiences in it) gazed upon with both wonder and knowledge. Whether she is considering a bird or a distant planet or a microbrew, Dean shows us multiple levels: A nature photograph, for example, is both conventional in its beauty, but awe-inspiring in the effort required to capture it. Somehow, *Fugitive Blues* moves us from the ordinary to the extraordinary, without leaving the ordinary behind. Quietly, these poems amaze.

—Philip Memmer, author of *The Storehouses of the Snow: Psalms, Parables, and Dreams*

FUGITIVE BLUES

Debra Kang Dean

Cover art: by Charli Barnes

ISBN: 978-0-913785-47-8

Interior pages designed by Charli Barnes

Moon City Press
Department of English
215 Siceluff Hall
Missouri State University
901 South National
Springfield, MO 65897
www.mooncitypress.com

ACKNOWLEDGMENTS

Grateful acknowledgment is made to the editors of the following print and online publications, where the following poems first appeared:

Connotation Press: An Online Artifact: "Lady's Slipper"
The Florida Review: "Blue Sky With Koi" and "Ode to the Brown-Headed Cowbird"
The Hampden-Sydney Review: "Juniper" and "Song"

"Punchbowl" appeared in *America! What's My Name?!: The "Other" Poets Unfurl the Flag*, Frank X. Walker, ed. (Nicholasville, KY: Wind Publications, 2007).

This is for my loved ones, now "gone altogether beyond." To my family and friends, and to my Spalding community, gratitude from one still finding her way.

TABLE OF CONTENTS

PUNCHBOWL

The light that puts out our eyes is darkness to us.
                                        —Thoreau

Here in this theater under the stars,
        Ernie Pyle's marked grave is only one
    among a thousand others simply marked "unknown."
        But long before they were all killed
        along the Pacific Rim, another drama unfolded,

    a bleak reminder of what seems
        the unkillable law: Some thing must die
    that others might live. Here was the place
        of sacrifice, the bodies of lawbreakers,
    drowned below in a pond, borne up to the crater

and placed on a stone slab—some left alone,
        some reduced to ash and bone that the family
    gathered up and carried home. On the slopes
        of this crater, I saw the after-effect of slaughter
    on a small scale—some mongoose or stray

        had found its way into my brother's pigeon coop
            and scattered the flock that never came back.
    Memory blinks, and the smell of pigeon shit, blood is
        conjured up, the featherless skin of hatchlings turning
    rubbery where they hung on perches or fell.

The road to the now-locked gate branches off to
        "homestead" land, so called so we can forget
    the place. They say the crater's extinct,
            the Pacific plate grinding steadily northward,
        but who can really know or say for sure what stirs

under the surface? The inexorable law of bodies
tells us no two can occupy the same space.
Some must leave that others might live. *Go back
where you came from.* But there's no there there
to return to. Tonight I have climbed from my father's house

up over the rim and descended into the crater to lie,
sober, among the dead. This glimpse of the past—
it's like looking at stars: Once you know what you're seeing,
the hour of innocence is past. The light of dying stars
puts out our eyes. Again and again in the dark,

we stumble. We stumble and fall. And yet,
as if certain we know where we are, we get up.

CONFESSIONAL

If you're holding the charts
that map out the constellations
while looking to name a few stars,
say, Altair, Vega, Aldebaran, or

if you're searching
for cartoonish explosions,
for remix or parody on the screen,
maybe this isn't for you.

I'm serious. (I've been told
I'm too serious.) Sorry. In truth,
I don't mean I'm sorry;
I just want an unlocked gate

to swing on the hinge of those words.
When I say I put down my cat last month,
I'm not talking about talking.
I mean I shut the gate. I mean

at four in the morning I woke to the sound
of distress—slow after nineteen years,
I did finally learn to hear it—
and held him through a seizure,

a fissure the self he was slipped through.
After which, for him, all of life was refusal.
I called the vet. I put him in the carrier
I called the Death Car after I put down
my other cat—to own my actions.

Don't ask me to name my cats.
If you're still with me, perhaps
you're thinking, *Christ, they're just cats.*

Well, after the fact, thought/said
some of the onlookers and virtual
onlookers watching two women
putting each other down, *Catfight.*

Bitch, one woman had said. *Fuck you.*
You're stupid, the other repeated. And then
the first punch. Then clawing and
a prying loose. *Christ, it's just a seat.*

It's a seat on the bus where
the people go 'round and 'round.
If you were listening, I think
you know what I mean. Perhaps

it's why we're unapologetic. I know
I'm being a hypocrite: This is
a virtual sound of grief turned
grievance—and that is my grief.

The last gasps rattle a body.
I know. Remember my cat?
Rumor has it departing souls
like the hottest stars burn blue.

In the language of fists,
it's red, a cheek flames red.
It's a sorry sight. Sorry,
I'm saying, Sorry.

BLUE SKY WITH KOI

As if to be in the heartland was not to be
        in the center but farthest removed
from every other point—I saw this first in Art
        Sinsabaugh's photographs: homesteads
        like islands, your green sea not yet risen to flood tide.

        Not my constant sea swayed by the moon
            but a sea of expectant ears, I imagined;
in the air the odor, the ordure, of pigs,
        and year after year that sea receding,
leaving the brittle spikes of corn stubble—

as if a rain of arrows launched toward
        heaven had broken against hard dirt. Only
    twenty years ago, I'm told, this I might have seen
        with my own eyes, just north of town
        where the college, an island continent,

        now sprawls. On this blue day, without
            a single cloud to parcel out the sky, I am
    remembering your huge hands held out
        under the waterfall that I might see
your not-yet-toddler baby girl turning her bright face,

eyes closed, away from you and toward
        the cool mist. There, inside the geodesic
    dome that is the Climatron, the familiar
            thick air pressed against each exposed pore;
        in the pungent air the faintly mildewy scent of

the home I am always but never quite leaving.
    Outside, paths in the Japanese garden, laid out
to conceal and reveal each new vista, bent and
    turned, keeping bad spirits a few steps behind us.
As if for a moment I had bathed my senses

in the floating world that memory keeps suspended
    just above this one. The day was cool and clear
and blue like this one, the slightly opaque water
    in the man-made pond still, so still, it gave us
back to ourselves as, silent, we stood on the bridge.

    But, of course, we knew such illusions can't last.
    Over the placid water you cast a handful of pellets
as if they were coins. The water roiled for an instant
    before a hundred carp troubled the water,
fins and tails propelling them forward and upward

to break the surface, each shouldering each, lipless mouths,
    like brittle parchment, fully extended, though whether
to utter a silent O or Oh, I couldn't tell. *That's chaos,*
    you said, clapping the residue of food from your hands
as the water began the slow work of righting itself,

as we sauntered back across the bridge, and, parting,
turned away and onward toward our separate lives.

ODE TO THE
BROWN-HEADED COWBIRD

Brood parasite of those passerines,
with your leatherlike hood,
your iridescent black body,

neither the plagiarist of the aviary nor
the sequined harlequins are as reviled
by lovers of songbirds as you are.

The notes of your song fall first like water's
then like a jackhammer's. You sing
and listen, wait for that come-hither

wing stroke, subtle as a Noh
gesture, draw closer, sing
a different melody, then again

draw closer. How many songs
have you sung, must you
sing for that brief cloacal kiss?

In this, your first season after
the plagues of failure, you will
finally taste success.

Forty eggs will your mate lay
each in a different nest—warbler's,
red-winged blackbird's, junco's ...

If not turned out or pecked open,
they will hatch offspring
already skilled in begging. And now,

reformed delinquent, from this day forward
free as a bird you will stay.
After a year perfecting technique

and learning to look and listen,
you have arrived, winged Philoctetes.
Who wouldn't envy you?

CROSSINGS: OIL ON CANVAS

after Maxine Yalovitz-Blankenship

—

Here's where I started:
this one small square
with its cryptic blank stare.

Where was I going? What
did I want? I wanted more
light to efface all shadow.

Laying a mix of color on thick—see,
here's where the first shapes emerged:
from the gouge, a horizon, a destination.

|

Up from the narrow bed
in the dim room, I rose.
A door opened. In spilled
night's deep hue. The door's
long edge was a charred match
stick, the wall's
indecisive blues —or was it
an unlit candle, constricted,
the black pupil of a cat's eye?

<==>

An accordion wall. A pleated shade.
In the dusky light parallel lines

—an equal sign?—above the pitch of
a brown roof. I stand inside the Kirlian flame

framed in the arrowhead of greater than.
Who wouldn't want a little shadow.

In a parallel universe my spectral self reads.
Already a crowd has gathered.

The docked ship is ready to sail.

▲

A roof's steep
pitch resembles
a field tent,
a cave's mouth.

Always the way out
is the way in. Always
at the threshold

the humble stoop,
circling the square.

●

Here is the
Earth seen from space,
a wintry moon ringed with ice,
a lunar eclipse, oh, once in a
blue moon, the sun eclipsed. A
solar flare, the sun obscured by
clouds, and here—a sun
you can stare and
stare at.

The Confetti
of White Writing

Laying a mix of color on thick
    I remember confetti.

    When the fountain

    pen's fluid ink failed,
I pressed its tip into the page—

    a rain of quick strokes.

Sometimes impressed
    on the verso: cryptic messages

from the toddler I was.

More Confetti

As a teen, I kneeled by the bed alone
in my room. Words constellated on
the pages of a blank book.
                                    Down-
stairs, in the living room, my father
thinking on his feet. He was wearing
his favorite blue shirt, wedging his
hands deep in his pants pockets. The
confetti his shoe prints made.
                        In another room,
                        my mother sat in
                        a plush red chair
                        reading a book.
                                    She had turned
                                    the TV around so
                                    it faced the wall.
                                    Her tightly coiled
                                    yellow shawl was
                                    a limp dunce cap.

><

In the dreamscape along the boulevard of stars
   a wall of trees on my right.
On my left the sun lighting wet, young leaves.
   If you closed your eyes,
here's what you'd see: fall blurring reds and yellows orange.
   Beyond where the black road dips
the red sky's a warning. All over
   it's summer, clear sky
where the road levels.

AFTER "AKA-FUJI"

When
berorin re-
placed fugitive
blues, outline yielded
to shapes the colors made.
A scatter of clouds far above
the tree line. No snow on the red
peak. High noon. From the south-
east, light winds. We have arrived, Old
Paint. Once more the mountains are mountains.

LADY'S SLIPPER

It's a pretty photograph,
I thought, decorative as
a silk rose in its neat frame

until I encountered
a photographer lugging
camera and tripod,

a bagful of lenses in muddy,
ankle-wrenching terrain—
roots and rocks, dips and stumps.

It had taken days of aimless
wandering, he said,
of simply looking ...

as now I remember your wonder
at those first photographs
beamed back from Spirit

and Opportunity. Far too driven
by deadlines, I stood
at your shoulder and stared

at the screen. What, I thought,
no moonsuits, no moon walking,
no one giant step as through

Spirit's lens we caught
a glimpse of Opportunity
looking rather insectlike,

we agreed, you clicking
slowly through the images
they gave us, in each

an eerie glow like the mercury-
vapor haze we'd seen
at 2 a.m., Dealy Plaza, 1975.

Mars, you said. *That's Mars.*

ODE TO BEER

If I think too hard, I could find it
pretty disturbing—my wandering the beer
aisle in search of my favorite microbrew
when he suddenly looms—a Hoosier, local,
I'm sure, big as a sumo wrestler—before
me. That I don't retreat is a test-
ament to my latest, and, no doubt, my best
round yet of self-medicating. I do admit
it *is* embarrassing being a woman, fifty-four,
haunting the beer section. Is that a sneer
I see before me? Fear makes me see yokels
everywhere since my friend was murdered. You
understand, I'm sure. *I'm looking for Robert the Bruce,*
I say, *Three Floyds out of Munster,* ask him to check,
tell him I was really hoping to be global buying local.
Together we walk the aisle and then he says, *Wait,*
and I follow him to the end cap. He's now clearly
on a mission. He disappears, reappears, offering
alternatives. As if touched by a godmother's wand—poof!
—this guy's turned aficionado, talking, nay, cooing
about the hops and body and sweetness of craft beers.
Whoa, you're serious, I interrupt. He blushes. In strictest
confidence, I tell him my granny bootlegged saké to get
the family through the war years. About then Procol
Harum's one hit starts piping in—another oldie
full of the heady infusions I now only sometimes long for.
He talks me through brews from Oregon to Massachusetts,
which brings him around to his own favorite brew
from Texas, which happens to be on sale. My guess

is, he likes the idea of this Old World beer as much as the beer.
My guess is, I won't like it. But that's not the point anymore.
You know, Shiner Bock isn't Scottish. And yet I've called
him out, and he has answered with a guarded hopefulness
I find disarming: *I hope you like it.* At home, before
I crack open the first of the six-pack, I'll google
Shiner, learn something about the Texans who craft it.
With beer, at least, I tell him as I leave, it isn't for-
ever, thinking maybe he isn't strictly local after all. You
just never know. Glancing back, he says, *That's the spirit.*

JUNIPER

Three days past the equinox,
here by a window, again,
reading *Eternity's Woods*
because you asked me to,
though, with my *somber
faith resembling
hope*, it isn't a river
and distant hills I see
but three pines, bare branches
of deciduous trees,
and one crow in a wash
of undivided blue.

For two days it had rained,
so it isn't hard to figure out
why only one bare tree,
a little sheltered by a pine,
is deeply tinged
with a leaf bud's coral.
Outside the window
a stop sign and farther out
across the parking lot
the stars-and-stripes measured
by the wind. Once I believed
in the permanence of mountains,
a wild horse against which
a man might test himself. Now
I know how fragile they are.
Now we break, we blast them
for a vein of coal.

Last week, flying into
the Springs, the sight
of snow-capped peaks
and there it was:
from deep within me
that audible indrawn breath
and the silence one hears
afterwards in the seemingly
inconsolable child—a chance
encounter drawing her back.
The next day, Fred and I
would walk the rimrock
of the outcropping
I stared and stared at
from the kitchen window.
It was that close.

Out past the oil rigs
and platforms, past
tires and plastic bottles,
the ATV tracks,
a makeshift campsite
draped in a sheet,
we walked. The first time
the trail dropped steeply,
he said, *Walk like a duck—*
short, wide steps
to slow you down.
I'd heard it before.

Falling in behind him,
I saw evidence
of the stroke, how
he lifted his right foot,
toe close to the ground
for a moment before
the heel touched down—
as a dog or coyote might.

Here was his esplanade
of wind and cliff edge
carved by water, where,
he told me, rock doves nest,
where jays might fly
from tree to scrubby tree
as if to light his walk.
When, pointing, I asked,
he gave me a name:
strawberry cactus.
He bent a little
to break off juniper needles,
rubbing them between his palms,
then lifting his cupped hands
up to my face
as if holding a bird
he'd plucked from the air.
Out here, he said,
in this high desert,
by reason of water,
of wind and soil,
no two give off
exactly the same scent.

There, the air so clear,
unaided he could hear
and speak beyond
the crabbed masculinity
of what he has been—
warrior and hunter, country
son of the ravaged city
of Flint, father of the man
I loved, who, now living
among the dead, yet
walks between us
when the trail levels,
sometimes holding our hands.
Even with all the stories I've heard,
what do I really know
of where they have been.

SONG

Goldfinches—they were—
not yellow leaves—four
drawn up
into the trees—a blur,
black-laced raw color
borne up.
I was thunked, word-stirred:
Sunlight, sunlight, bird.

Willow, widow, her-
self, my self once more
borne out,
in the late light shorn
from summer forward
drawn out:
not yellow leaves—four
goldfinches they were.

ABOUT THE AUTHOR

Debra Kang Dean is the author of two books and two chapbooks of poetry. She has also published essays, most recently in the expanded edition of *The Colors of Nature: Culture, Identity, and the Natural World* and *Until Everything Is Continuous Again: American Poets on the Recent Work of W.S. Merwin.* She teaches in the brief-residency MFA in Writing Program at Spalding University and currently lives in Bloomington, Indiana.